How to Draw Birds

by Anna Betts

www.bsmall.co.uk

Contents

About the illustrations
The artist who put this book together has developed an advanced technique that uses a computer to add effects and colours to her drawings. This makes the illustrations really clear and easy to copy. If you do not have a computer at home then you can add colour by hand. In fact, this is what we expect you to do! Do not worry if your drawing is different to the ones in this book—they are your drawings.

How to use this book

The techniques in this book will teach you how to draw birds. The techniques get harder as you go through the book so start at the beginning to build up your skills.

By the end of the book, you will be drawing fanciful characters and texture-filled birds of all kinds.

There are a few skills that you will need before you can start some of the exercises.

Tracing

1. Place a piece of tracing paper over the drawing that you want to use.
2. Trace the outline of the image that you have chosen.
3. Turn the tracing paper over and scribble over the outline on the other side.
4. Then turn the tracing paper back over—the scribbled side should be facing down—and trace the outline again on to a piece of blank paper.

Copying

If the activity asks you to copy something then you can either trace it or you can draw it slowly on your own. You will need lots of practice to do this but if you observe the image carefully then it can be done.

Rubbings

1. Find a texture that you want to take a rubbing of. For example, wood, concrete or a wall.
2. Hold your paper against your chosen surface.
3. Using wax, a crayon or a colouring pencil, rub on the paper and the texture from the surface below will appear. You can do this on to a blank piece of paper or directly on to your drawing, if you are careful.

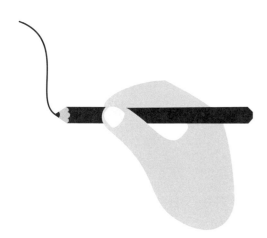

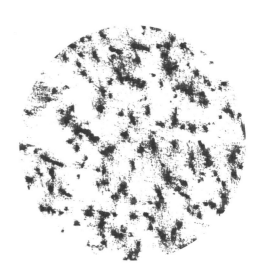

Curves

Most birds have lots of curves in their bodies, wings and beaks. By dividing the bird into curved lines, you can build up your drawing piece by piece.

1. Start with this flamingo's long, smooth neck. Follow the curve.

2. Pick out the other curves as shown to make the body.

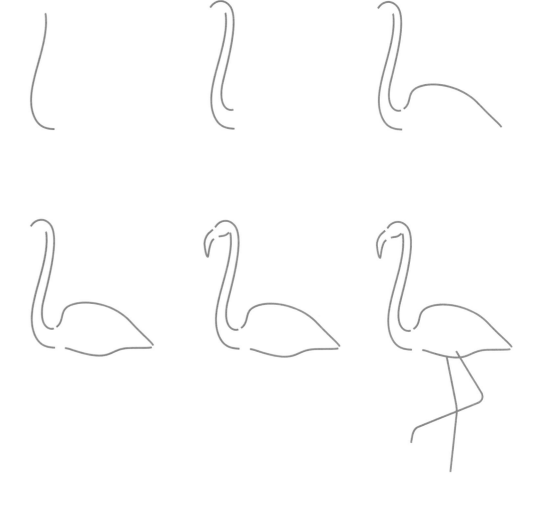

3. Now that you have the basic shape, you can add details like the eye, beak, legs and feathers. See the example for some help.

4. Flamingos are bright pink because of the food that they eat. Add some colour to your drawing and draw a background.

Tip: Flamingos like water!

Negative space

Looking at the spaces between shapes, instead of at the shapes themselves, is a great way to notice all of the details. This area is called the 'negative space'.

1. Focus on the colourful part of the drawing here. This is the negative space around the bird. Using this, you will be able to create the hummingbird in the centre.

2. Starting from the edge of the page, draw some straight lines towards the centre using a light pencil, like in the image opposite.

3. Using colouring pencils, create each colourful shape one after the other, leaving the white shape in the centre blank.

4. The hummingbird will come together like a jigsaw puzzle. You can now fill your bird with colour and patterns.

Tip: Hummingbirds live in hot countries and come in all sorts of bright colours, so let your imagination run wild!

Circles

Groups of circles, ovals and other curved shapes can come together to make the basic outline of a bird. Puffins have nice round bodies and are a good example of a bird that you can draw using this technique. You could also use this method to draw owls, pigeons and chickens.

1. Start with a circle for the head and an oval—a bit like a squashed circle—for the body. Puffins have quite large heads for a bird.

2. Join the head and body together with curves. This is the neck.

3. Now draw the beak, tail and feet. Curved shapes will look more natural than straight lines.

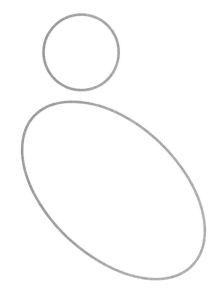

4. Once you have a good outline you can draw the detail. Puffins have very expressive eyes—they are like a rounded triangle—and their beaks are unusual, too.

Tip: Other names for puffins include 'clowns of the sea' and 'sea parrots' because of their colourful markings. So you can use lots of colours.

Scaling grid

A scaling grid breaks up an image into squares. Each square contains some detail from the image. Working from square to square, you can copy the detail to another grid. Change the size of your image by using bigger or smaller squares, as long as the grid has the same number of squares.

1. Here is a grid of squares drawn over an image of a kingfisher.

2. Copy the grid on the opposite page on to a blank piece of paper. See page 3 for instructions.

3. Look carefully at the kingfisher on this page and start to draw the details on your grid using a pencil. Press lightly in case you need to rub anything out.

4. Think about the shapes made in each square by the kingfisher's outline. Some squares will be blank and some will be full.

5. Once you have created the outline, you can rub out the grid lines and start to add colour. Draw in the details to make your kingfisher.

Materials

When drawing, the tools that you use are just as important as your technique. There are lots of pens, pencils and other drawing materials to choose from.
You will need to think about what you need for your picture.

Thickness

Thick lines are good for outlines and important features. Thin lines are good for detail.

Strength

Hard lines will suit still objects and soft lines will help to show movement.

Texture

Some tools make solid lines and others will create a scratchy effect.

Colour

Colouring pens will look different to colouring pencils or even chalk.

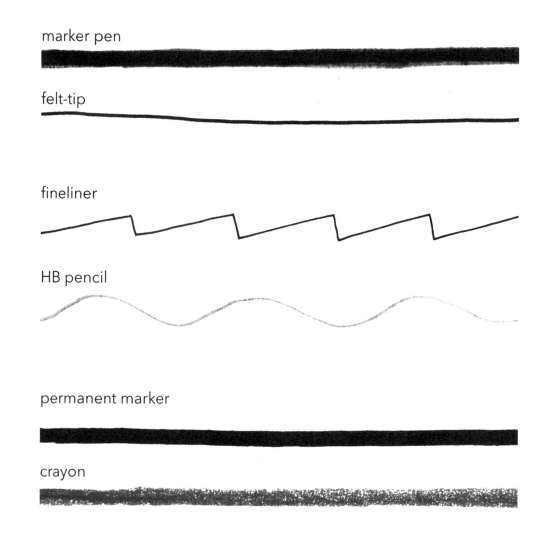

marker pen

felt-tip

fineliner

HB pencil

permanent marker

crayon

colour pencil

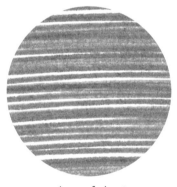

colour felt-tip

colour paint

The best way to learn about materials is to practise with them. Experiment to find out which tools give you the effect you want and which tools you enjoy using.

1. Trace this feather following the instructions on page 3.

2. Use different pens and pencils to draw over the outline.

3. Fill the shape with colour using pencils, pens or paint.

Which do you prefer?

3D shading

Shading helps to make objects look more realistic. The shadows will be darker or lighter depending on where the light is coming from.

1. Trace or copy these shapes so that you can practise shading.

2. Choose the right kind of tool for the job. You will need a pencil.

3. There are three strengths of grey in these shapes: light, medium and dark. The arrows show where the light is coming from. You can see that the side hidden from the light is darker.

4. For the cube, press gently with the pencil for the lighter areas and press heavily for the darker areas. Shade from side to side.

5. For the sphere, shade using circular motions. You can do a light layer first and then add the darker shadows afterwards.

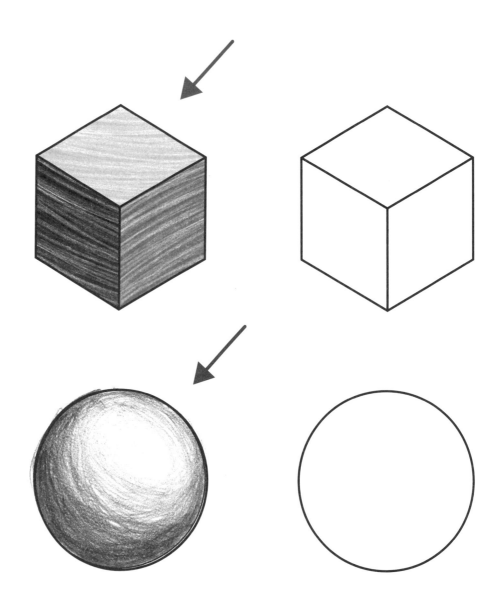

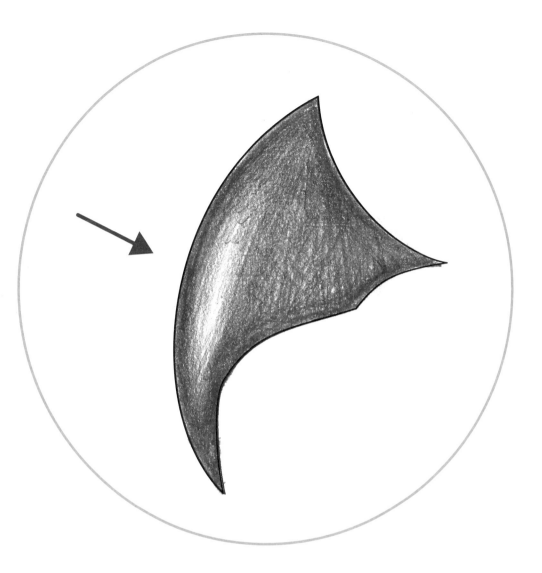

Once you have mastered the skill of shading, trace the outline of this beak and add the shadows. The red arrow shows where the light is coming from.

When drawing birds, the shading of the beak is important because it is one of the few parts of the bird not covered in feathers. The eyes and feet are other parts of the bird that will also reflect the light clearly.

Try moving the light source to the opposite side and shading the beak. Which bits will be lighter and which bits will be darker?

Geometric outlines

Birds have many unusual features such as beaks, tails and feathers. By dividing up the image into geometric shapes—such as triangles, squares and other shapes with hard corners—you can make sure these features are all the right size and in the correct place.

This technique is a useful way to draw a bird for the first time. There are many ways to divide up an image with geometric shapes. Here are some examples using popular birds to get you started.

1. Copy the geometric patterns on to a blank piece of paper using a pencil and pressing gently so that you can rub them out later.

2. Draw the details in and around the shapes. You can use a different coloured pencil here to help separate your drawing from the shapes.

3. Rub out the geometric shapes.

4. Draw in the details and add some colour to your bird.

Patterns

There are many beautiful patterns in nature and birds are no exception. This peacock's wonderful tail is a fantastic example of one.

Patterns are attractive but difficult to create without careful planning. Here are some tips to help you bring some natural flair to your drawings.

1. Trace or copy the image from the opposite page.

2. Study the peacock's tail. Look at the spacing between the shapes, at the size of them and how often they repeat themselves.

3. Practise drawing the detail from the box on the right so that you are ready to add the pattern to the peacock's tail.

4. Starting at the peacock's body and working towards the edge, use a pencil to add the shapes before you add any detail. Make sure they are the right size.

5. Draw in the detail and add the colour to complete your pattern.

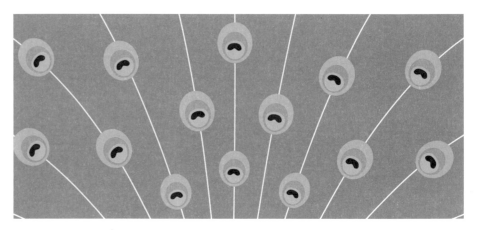

Trace or copy this image.

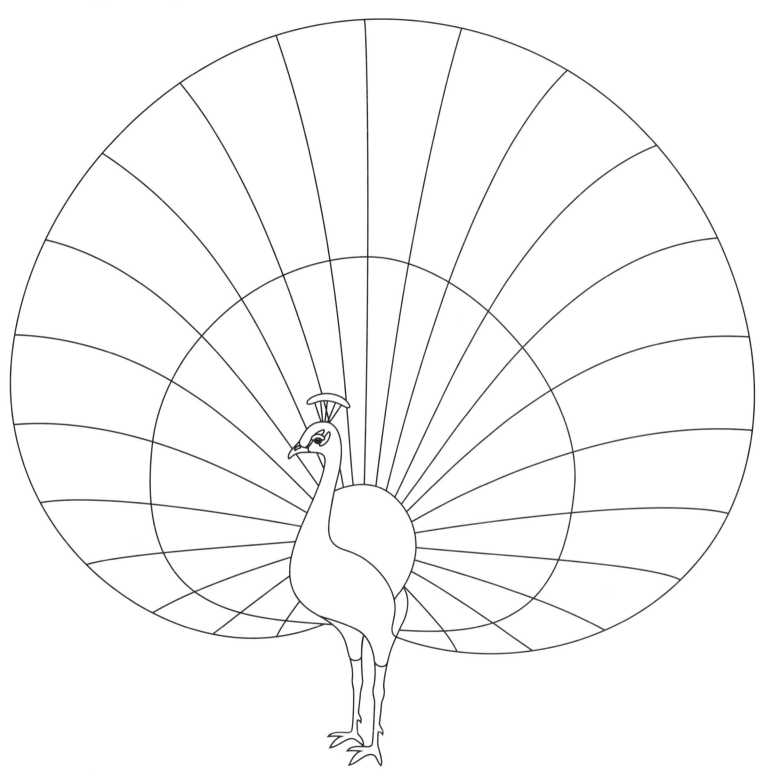

Texture

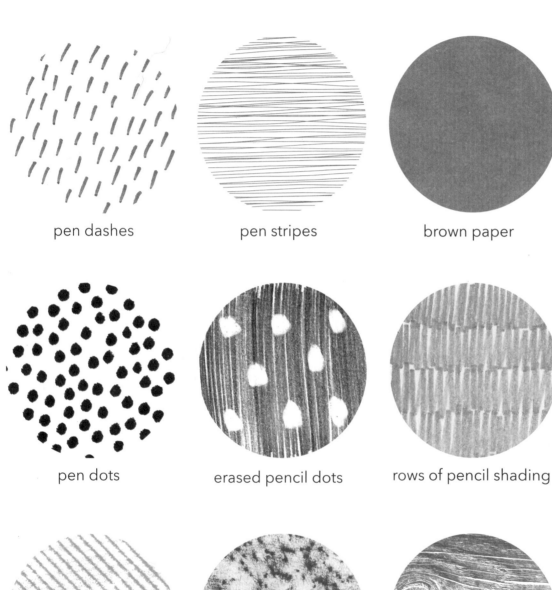

pen dashes

pen stripes

brown paper

pen dots

erased pencil dots

rows of pencil shading

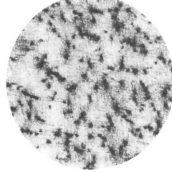

cardboard rubbing

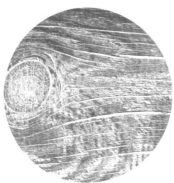

concrete rubbing

wood rubbing

There are hundreds of different textures that you can experiment with. Here are a few examples of textures that will help you to draw your bird.

You can create texture by using a variety of materials. Think about whether you need a smooth texture or a rough texture. This will make your drawing more interesting.

Try to collect a page full of these different textures using the materials that you have. See page 3 for instructions.

1. Trace or copy this image.

2. Use the techniques on the opposite page to add texture to your bird.

Tip: You can create a realistic bird or a fantasy bird. What would this bird look like with a wooden texture on the wings?

In motion

Taking off

Birds are often standing still in drawings but in real life they have the amazing ability to fly. It is difficult to draw birds in motion because you have to think about the position of their body, feet, wings and head.

Here, you can see examples of this bird holding on to a branch, taking off and flying high in the sky. The following steps will help you to create your own bird in motion.

1. Look at the wings. Are they straight or curved, are they open or tucked away?

2. Draw the head from the correct angle. Are you looking at it from the side or from below?

Use your imagination to make sense of your drawing. Is the bird taking off or landing? Is the bird hungry or happy or scared?

View from below

Waiting on a branch

Colour mixing

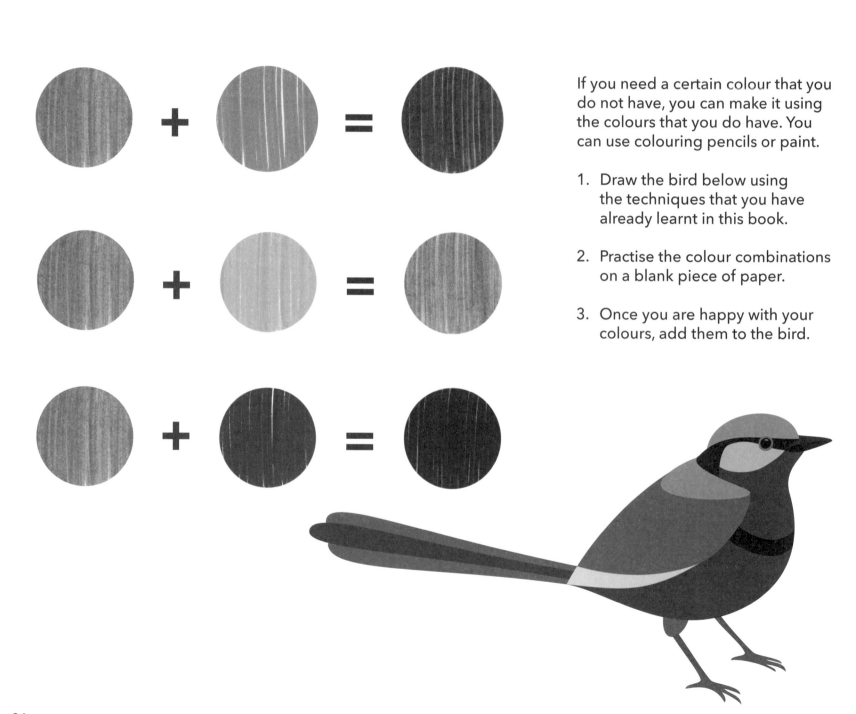

If you need a certain colour that you do not have, you can make it using the colours that you do have. You can use colouring pencils or paint.

1. Draw the bird below using the techniques that you have already learnt in this book.

2. Practise the colour combinations on a blank piece of paper.

3. Once you are happy with your colours, add them to the bird.

This bird is very colourful so you will need some more complicated colour combinations.

Follow the steps on the opposite page but use the colour combinations on this page when you practise.

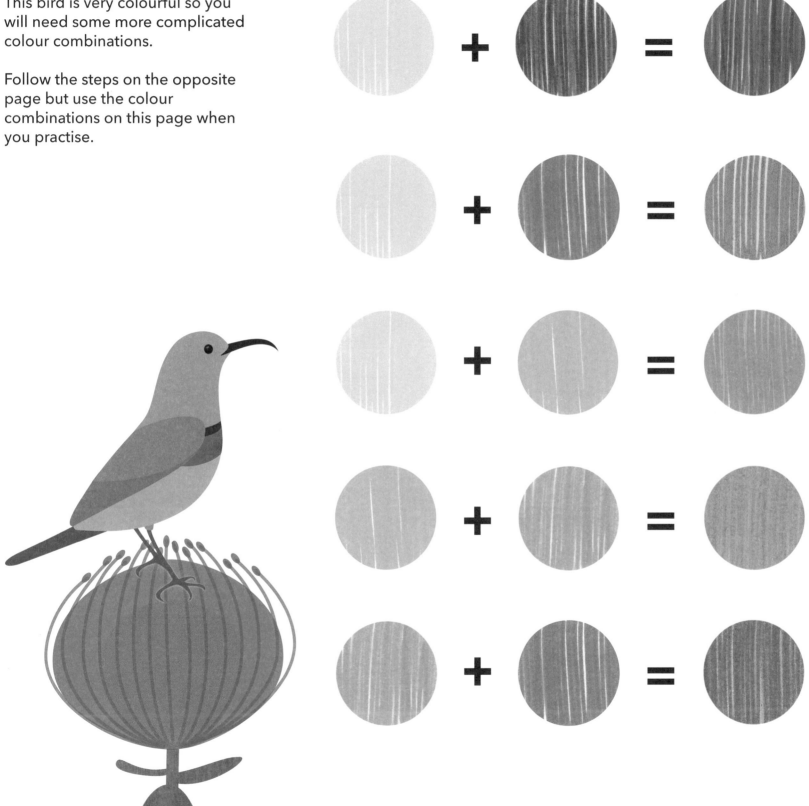

Line drawings

A line drawing is full of detail and has no colour. Lines are used to show the different parts of the bird such as the wing, the eye and the patches of coloured feathers. For a technical drawing, you should use a thin, smooth line. You can read about adding character on page 28.

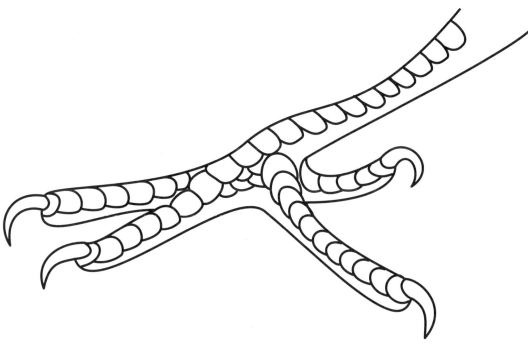

1. Work backwards from a colourful picture like the woodpecker on the opposite page.

2. Look for the boundaries between the different colours and use a line to separate them.

3. Select an interesting detail such as the feet and draw them on their own. Add lots of detail.

Drawing characters

Now is your chance to flex those creative muscles. Drawing a character is all about telling a story. Think about the main features of your chosen bird. This owl, for example, has big eyes and a fat little body. In stories, owls are often clever characters—they are wise, sensible and maybe a little bit unfriendly to people.

1. Use the techniques in the book to create a line drawing of the owl. You could use a combination of the circles technique on page 8 and the curves technique on page 4.

2. This time, draw it again and exaggerate the main features. Give your owl bigger eyes or a big head. Leave out the features that you do not need to create your character.

3. Once you are happy with your owl drawing, you can add human features or clothing to make your character. The owl opposite is wearing glasses and a moustache to make him look like a detective!

4. Trace or copy the simple line drawing above. Add different features and experiment with characters.

There are plenty of birds throughout this book that you could turn into characters. For example, the puffin on page 9 might make a good clown. Or the flamingo on page 5 could be an athlete wearing a sweatband.

Once you have created your character, write a short story about him or her. What are they doing?

Inspiration

Birds lay their **eggs** in a **nest**, which they make from twigs, moss and even spider's webs.

This **mandarin duck** has a fascinating swirl of colourful feathers.

Many birds will perch on a **branch** to rest.

Pelicans are famous for their large bills, which they use to scoop up fish from water.

Trees provide homes to many types of birds. They also provide shelter and food.

Kiwi are a small bird from New Zealand. They have tiny wings and cannot fly. Their feathers are more like fur.

Published by b small publishing ltd.
Text and illustrations © b small publishing ltd. 2016   1 2 3 4 5 6 7 8 9 10
British Library Cataloguing-in-Publication Data: A catalogue record for this book is available from the British Library.
Illustrations: Anna Betts   Design: Anna Betts   Editorial: Sam Hutchinson   Production: Madeleine Ehm
Printed in China by WKT Co. Ltd.   ISBN 978-1-909767-85-0
Please visit our website if you would like to contact us.

www.bsmall.co.uk